Lorenzo Morandi

The Weekender

# TURIN

COLLECTIVE SHORTS
*by* NHP PUBLISHING

"I dedicate this book to my travel companion Sara, published on our tenth wedding anniversary" – Lorenzo

It often happens that places do not live up to the image formed through their representations, offering a less beautiful reality. Turin has the opposite effect on me and many visitors, revealing a reality better than the external image.

A state capital for three centuries, Turin is a city that has earned respect through its monumental constructions, elegant architecture, urban layout, and power buildings. This "courteously assertive" style guided the political-military unification of Italy. Turin is also the city that first initiated the industrialization process, triggering significant demographic and urban changes. For decades, the emphasis on its scientific-industrial character caused Turin to downplay its landscape, artistic, and cultural resources in the eyes of the outside world, as if these were less important or even detrimental to the idea of a highly productive city.

What particularly fascinates me is Turin's attitude compared to other cities that are better at projecting an image of themselves, almost as if it has an inferiority complex. On the other hand, I am convinced that today the city is asserting a vision capable of dispelling the idea of an introverted city. What emerges is a plurality of perspectives that can transform culture from mere ornament and theatrical backdrop into a path of development and reaffirmation. I like to transfer this idea onto the physical and material reality of the city itself, where monumental and solemn buildings and grand squares are now living elements, actively engaging with contemporary times through new uses, hybridizations, and transformations.

Turin is the capital of Piedmont and is less than 100 km from where I live, just an hour by train. It is the setting for my most important artistic and professional interactions and collaborations, a testament to how the city is fertile ground for the development and exchange of ideas. The photographs depicting the four days spent in Turin in this book cannot and do not aim to present a unified and definitive vision of the city, but rather offer free and evocative itineraries, where visits to some of the most well-known places of interest are interspersed with less conventional stops. The images are fragments of one of the infinite trajectories that can be undertaken, traversing epochs, fashions, styles, and tastes, discovering the city without prejudice and with sincere curiosity, ready to change direction following instinct.

Lorenzo Morandi

# Thursday

Arrival at Porta Nuova Station Thursday 2:30 PM

35
OPERA
BOUTIQUE HOTEL
35
OPERA
BOUTIQUE HOTEL

35 OPERA
BOUTIQUE HOTEL

Checking in at Opera35 Boutique Hotel

Thursday 3:10 PM

Thursday 3:50 PM

The first city sights

Fontana del Po

Thursday 4:50 PM

Fontana della Dora

De Crustatis Lib. II.
DE CANCRIS IN GENERE.
Cap. XVI.
ÆQVIVOCA.

H B
N A T
T R L P
F O D E
L N A P F

# Friday

Friday 9:20 AM Breakfast at Opera35 Boutique Hotel

MUSEO
NAZIONALE
RISORGIMENTO
ITALIANO

Friday 10:05 AM

Visiting Museo del Risorgimento

Exploring the city center

Friday 12:10 PM

TORINO
SPAZIO AL
FUTURO

LUX

Friday 1:15 PM

Farinata at Padellino Factory

Visiting Casa Mollino

Friday 2:20 PM

16
2879

Friday 3:50 PM

Moving to Superga

Gipsoteca Mondazzi

Friday 6:30 PM

Galleria Tina Biazzi Liberty & Deco

Friday 6:50 PM

Friday 8:40 PM

Dinner at Orma

BAROLO
FOGLIATI
LANGHE
80
30/35
ALTARE
RINALDI
24/29
23/33
23/28
31/36
24/26
FORAVIA
TOMMASO
ANCARANI
MACCHIONA
NEBBIA IN VALLE
33/38
65

## Saturday

Marocchino at Caffè Elena

Saturday 9 AM

The city that awakens

Saturday 9:30 AM

LETTERATURA CLASSICA
MOBILI D'ARTE
DONATELLO
LIBRI IN LINGUA

Saturday 9:45 AM

Bookstands in Via Po

TORINO
FUTURO

Visit Palazzo Reale e Musei Reali Saturday 10:10 AM

Saturday 12:40 PM

Lunch at Il Mannarino

Bicerin at Baratti e Milano Saturday 4:45 PM

Baratti & Milano

NEZ
NEZ
NEZ
NEZ
NEZ
NEZ
NEZ
NEZ

Saturday 5:10 PM

Laboratorio Olfattivo

Pista 500, Pinacoteca Agnelli

Saturday 6:10 PM

Saturday 6:50 PM

Sunset on the rooftop of Lingotto

CEDRATA

## Sunday

Breakfast at Cabaret Pasticceria Sunday 9:10 AM

Sunday 9:50 AM On the banks of the Po River

Sunday 10:40 AM

Borgo Medievale

VIA
BELFIORE
BOTTIGLIERIA
CUCINA
LOVERS

Lunch at Caffè dell'Orologio Sunday 12:45 PM

Art Nouveau architecture

Sunday 3:40 PM

Leaving the city

Sunday 5:20 PM

IL TER-RAZ-ZO
Metropolitana di Torino Linea 1
Biglietteria/Tickets

The Weekender

# TURIN

Published by New Heroes & Pioneers
Photography & text: Lorenzo Morandi
Creative Direction: Francois Le Bled
Series Book Design: Daniel Zachrisson
Edition Book Design: Lilith Onyett
Model: Sara Marini

Print and bound by BALTO print (Lithuania)
Legal deposit December 2024
ISBN 9789198656558

MIX
Paper | Supporting responsible forestry
FSC® C107574
FSC www.fsc.org



Opera35 Boutique Hotel - opera35.com
Circolo dei Lettori - circololettori.it
White Lands & Rare Books - whitelands.it
Paltò - paltotorino.it
Museo del Risorgimento - museorisorgimentotorino.it
Padellino Factory - padellinofactory.it
Casa Mollino - carlomollino.org/museo-casa-mollino
Gipsoteca Mondazzi - gipsoteca.it
Galleria Tina Biazzi
Liberty & Deco - libertyartnouveau.com

Orma - ormabistrot.it
Caffè Elena - caffeelena.it
Palazzo Reale - ilpalazzorealeditorino.it
Il Mannarino - ilmannarino.it
Teatro Regio di Torino - teatroregio.torino.it
Baratti e Milano - barattiemilano.it
Laboratorio Olfattivo - laboratorioolfattivo.com
Pinacoteca Agnelli - pinacoteca-agnelli.it
Cabaret Pasticceria - cabaretpasticceria.it
Caffè dell'Orologio - caffedellorologio.net

**COLLECTIVE SHORTS**
*by* NHP PUBLISHING